Complete the numbers to 20. Coun down.

1	2	3	4	5	6	7			
11	12	13	14	15	16	17	18	19	20	✓

Help the child to line up units under units and tens under tens, e.g.

9	10
19	20

Put the right number in the boxes and then draw the correct number of candles on each cake.

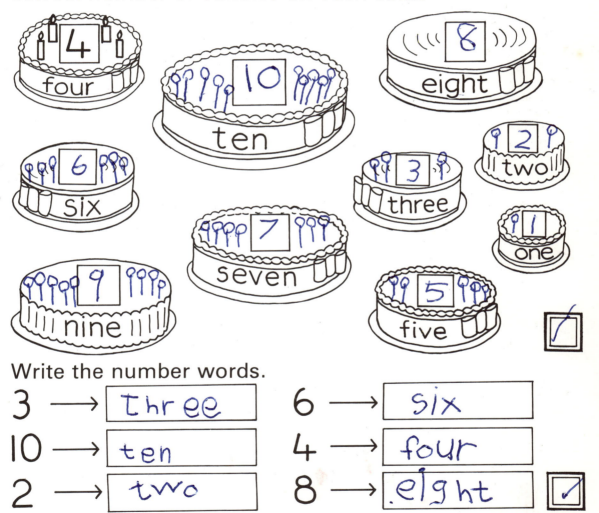

Write the number words.

3 → three   6 → six
10 → ten   4 → four
2 → two   8 → eight ✓

MORE TO DO: Make a set of number cards from scrap paper [0] [1] [2] etc. to ten and a set of word cards [one] [two]. Use these for matching, copying, tracing, etc. Play 'Which number?' – one partner spells out a number word whilst the other says which number has been spelt.

Complete the number line to nought. Start at 17 and count back.

| 0 | 1 | 2 | 3 | 4 | 5 | 6 | 7 | 8 | 9 | 10 | 11 | 12 | 13 | 14 | 15 | 16 | 17 | 18 | 19 | 20 |

Draw eleven rolls in the basket.

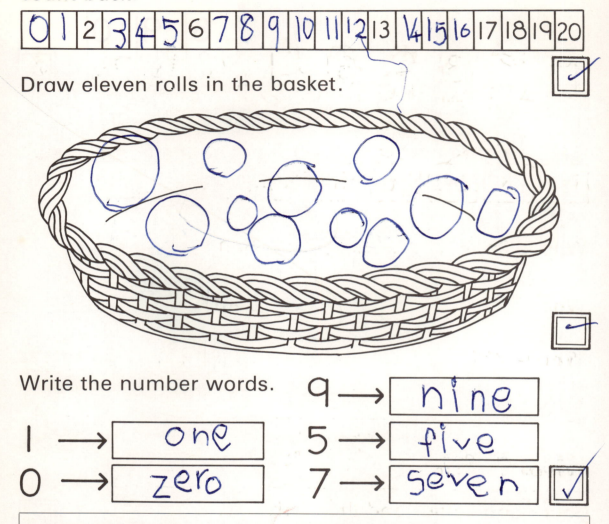

Write the number words.

1 → one
0 → zero
9 → nine
5 → five
7 → seven

Allow the child to copy the words if necessary. This will help towards being able to spell the words from memory. 0 can either be nothing, nought, or zero.

Colour the snake which has eleven stripes.

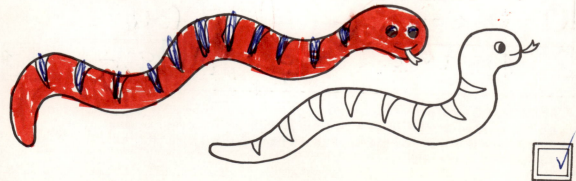

Count the people in the queue. How many?

Who is 2nd? ...tina... Ann is ...3rd...

Who is 9th? ...paul... Tom is ...1st...

Who is 4th? ...Bob... Jo is ...6th...

Make a queue of toys and then pick up the first, third, sixth, etc. The child can re-order the queue and tell you the new order – Action Man is first, Mini Metro is second, doll is third, and so on.

Count and colour and then write.

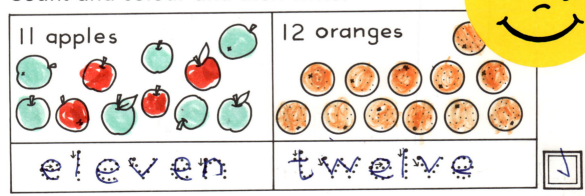

MORE TO DO: Draw pictures of eleven or twelve things. Practise writing eleven/twelve in crayon, felt pen, chalk, sand. Talk about the *first* day of the week, the *second* child in the family, the *fourth* knob (on the television) from the right/left, etc.

Fill in the missing numbers.

0 1 2 3 4 5 6 7 8 9 10 11 12 13 14 15 16 17

> Count aloud together first before the child fills in the numbers. If she is interested, tell her that all the missing numbers were odd numbers.

Tie a balloon to each number.

① ② ③ ④ ⑤ ⑥ ⑦ ⑧ ⑨ ⑩ ⑪ ⑫ ⑬

How many balloons? 13

Draw thirteen tadpoles in this pond.

Copy.

13 → thirteen

13 → thirteen

> Talk about thirteen being ten and three. It looks like a one and a three but the one means one ten. Remind the child to start at the dot and follow the arrow.

Draw fourteen socks on this washing line.

Write a number line to 15.

What is the number before 14?

What is the number after 14?

> Ask this question about other numbers in the line to help fix the position of the number in the child's mind.

Count and colour and then write.

> Check that the child is holding the pencil correctly (see *A note to parents* at the beginning of the book) and that the letters are being formed in the direction of the arrows.

Complete the 'add one' arrows to 14 and fill in the missing numbers.

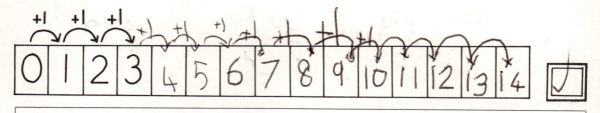

Help the child to count aloud 'nothing add one is one, one add one is two', etc. Test each other 'six add one is...?'

Can you do these sums?

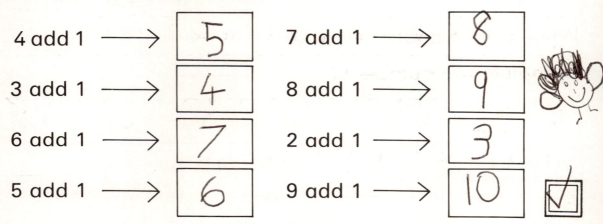

Add one brick to each tower. How many now?

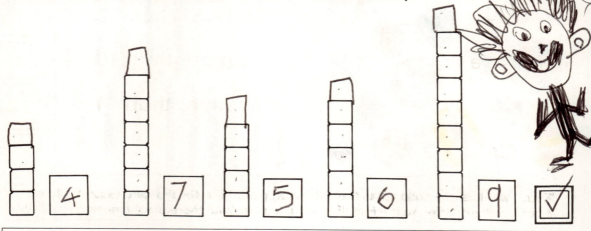

Repeat this exercise using real bricks.
  MORE TO DO: How many now? Make a collection of household objects then add one more, e.g. collect four forks, put them on table, add one more and then ask 'How many now?'

Adding on one is the same as saying <u>one more than</u>.
Put <u>one more</u> bead on each string. How many now?

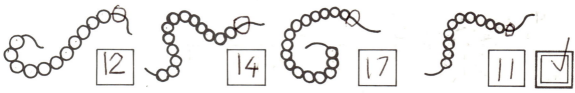

Put <u>one more</u> marble in each bag. How many now?

> If possible repeat these activities using real beads and marbles.

Complete the number line.

0 1 2 3 4 5 6 7 8 9 10 11 12 13 14 15 16 17 18 19 20

Use the number line to find out

one more than 7 → 8   one more than 17 → 18

one more than 4 → 5   one more than 14 → 15

one more than 2 → 3   one more than 12 → 13

one more than 0 → 1   one more than 10 → 11

one more than 1 → 2   one more than 11 → 12 ✓

> Notice whether the child spots the relationship between the first and second column. If not, draw attention to the fact that each number (and therefore the answer) in the second column is ten more than the corresponding number/answer in the first column.
>   MORE TO DO: Quick fire questions: one partner calls a series of numbers and the other partner immediately replies with the next consecutive number, e.g. five/six, three/four.

Complete the number line, then count aloud up and down.

0 1 2 3 4 5 6 7 8 9 10 11 12 13 14 15 16 17

What is the number before 16?   15

What is the number after 16?   17

Colour.   16

Start at the dot and tick sixteen boxes.

Start at the dot and tick seventeen boxes.

Count and colour and then write.

16 flowers — sixteen

17 flowers — seventeen

Check that the child is holding the pencil correctly and is following the direction of arrows.
  MORE TO DO: One partner claps or taps at slow pace, the other is asked to call 'now' when 16 (or any given number) is reached.

Add a ten to all the numbers in the bottom line to complete the numbers to 20.

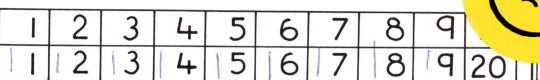

Explain that a ten, in this case, looks like a one as in <u>1</u>4. Point out the pattern of 4 + <u>10</u> = <u>1</u>4, 7 + <u>10</u> = <u>1</u>7, etc.

Colour ten balls.

How many balls altogether?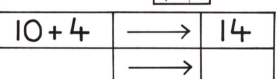

Copy the sum.

Do the sum.

Colour ten balloons.

How many balloons altogether? 12

Copy the sum.

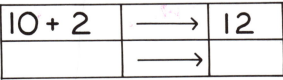

Do the sum.

Colour ten lemons.

How many lemons altogether? | 15 | ✓

Copy the sum.   10 + 5 → 15   → 15

Do the sum   5 + 10 → 15   15 ✓

> Point out the connection between the sum and the picture. Use your voice to stress 10+6 = <u>s</u>ixteen, 10+7 = <u>seven</u>teen.

Draw more flowers to make this into a bunch of thirteen flowers.

How many flowers did you draw? | 3 | ✓

Do the sums.   10 + 3 → 13   3 + 10 → 13

Write the numbers.

fourteen → 14   seventeen → 17

sixteen   → 16   eighteen → 18 ✓

> **MORE TO DO:** Make some '10' cards 18 10+8 . The caller says 'give me the eighteen card' and the 'picker' has to pick out the card which shows the sum 10+8. When you are the 'picker' make the occasional deliberate mistake for the child to correct.

Fill in the missing numbers, then count all the numbers aloud. Start at 8.

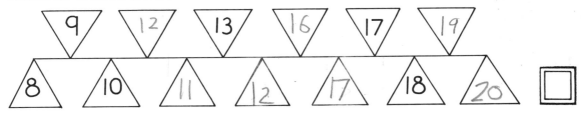

It is a good idea to vary the starting point of the number line. This forces the child to think about it in a different way and therefore strengthens the number concepts.

Write the number before 18.   Colour.

Write the number after 18.

Start at the dot and draw eighteen crosses.

Start at the dot and draw nineteen crosses.

Count the crosses together, then separately. Count aloud and touch each cross as you count.

Count and colour and then write.

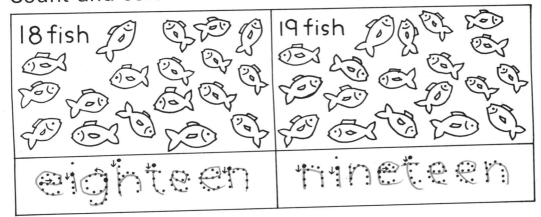

11

Complete the 'one less' arrows and fill in the missing numbers.

1 less 1 less

8 9 10 11 12 13 14 15 16 17 18 19 20

> Help the child to say aloud 'twenty less one is nineteen, nineteen less one is eighteen', etc. Omit the words '1 less', if necessary.

Can you do these sums?

one less than 13 → 12   one less than 6 → 5

one less than 12 → 11   one less than 4 → 3

one less than 10 → 9   one less than 5 → 4

one less than 9 → 8   one less than 7 → 6

> If possible, repeat the following activities using real coins and bricks.

Cross out one coin from each purse. How many now?

6   11   13   17

Cross out one brick from each tower. How many now?

6   5   8   7   10

> **MORE TO DO:** Complete 'backwards' number lines starting from any number, i.e. not always twenty.

One less than is the same as saying <u>take one from</u>.
Take one apple from each bowl. How many now?

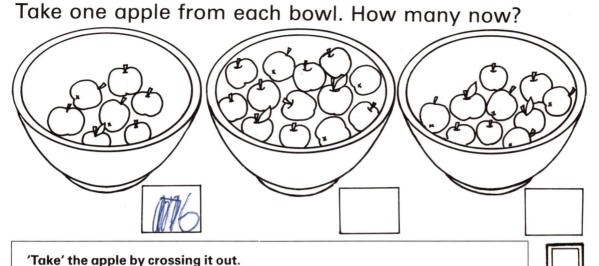

16

'Take' the apple by crossing it out.

Start from 16 and fill in the rest of the number line.

8 9 10 11 12 13 14 15 16

Point out that the number line is filled in by writing the number which is one less than the previous number.

Take one from.

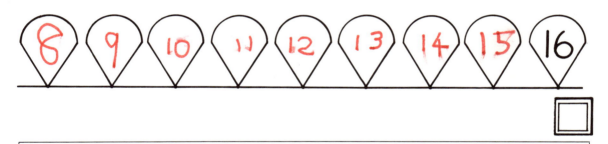

9 → 8   2 →   14 →
5 →   19 →   12 →
4 →   15 →

MORE TO DO: Make cards `1 less` `1 more` `add 1` . One partner calls a number and the other holds up the cards in random order – the caller has to keep on calling the right number for one minute, e.g. 'three' `1 less` 'two' `1 more` 'three' `add 1` 'four' `1 more` 'five' `1 less` 'four', and so on.

Fill in the missing numbers.

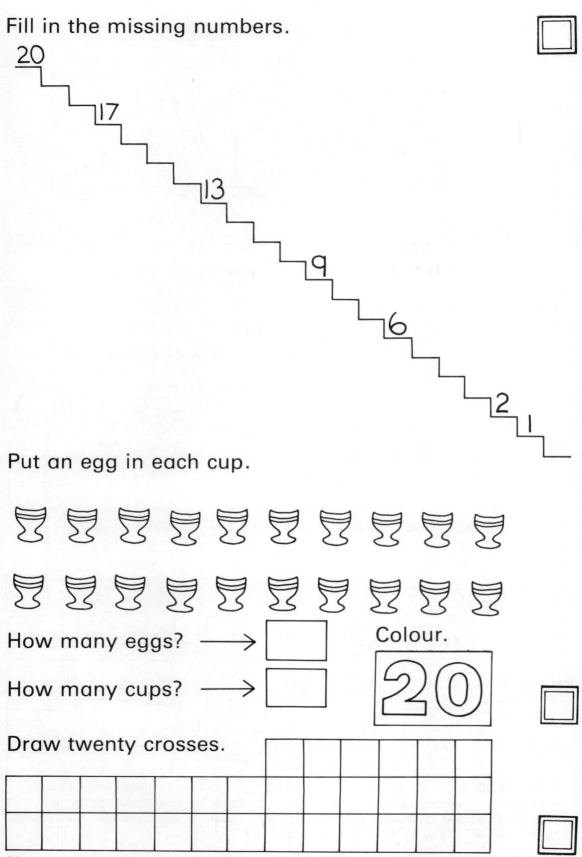

Put an egg in each cup.

How many eggs? →
How many cups? →

Colour.
20

Draw twenty crosses.

Count and colour, and then write.

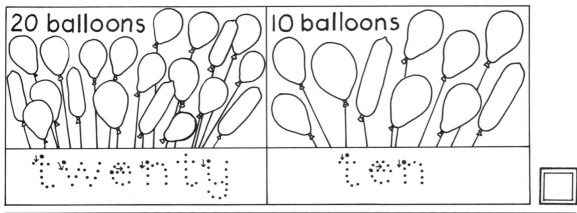

Check that the child is holding the pencil correctly and that the letters are being formed in the right direction.

Fill in the numbers on the number steps.

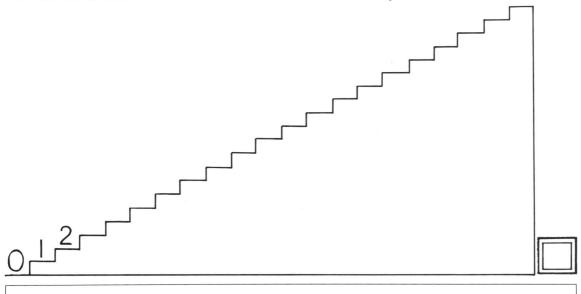

Count aloud *down* then up the steps to vary the usual order.

What number comes <u>before</u>?

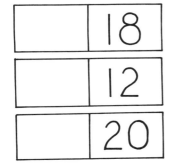
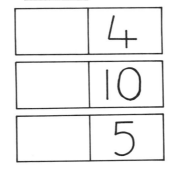
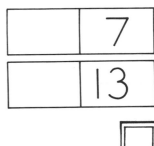

Count the flowers. How many? ☐

Colour the 1st flower red
Colour the 4th flower blue
Colour the 11th flower pink
Colour the 8th flower yellow

Draw a cross in every <u>second</u> box.

How many boxes altogether? ☐
How many crosses did you draw? ☐

Talk about the fact that in marking every second thing you in effect have halved the total number.

Colour the second person.

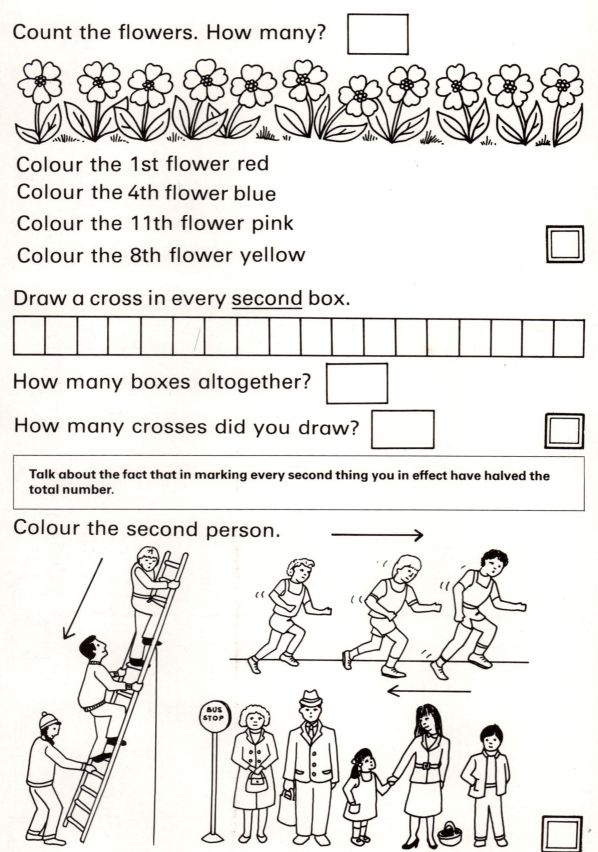

Draw a number line to 16. Start at nought and circle every _second_ number.

0 1 2 3 4 5 6 7 8 9 10 11 12 13 14 15

> Count aloud first the circled numbers then the others. Talk about odd and even numbers, look for examples around the house: clock faces, magazine pages, etc.

Put even numbers on the doors of these houses.

Put odd numbers on the doors of these houses.

Draw an even number of sweets in each bag.
Write the number of sweets you have drawn.

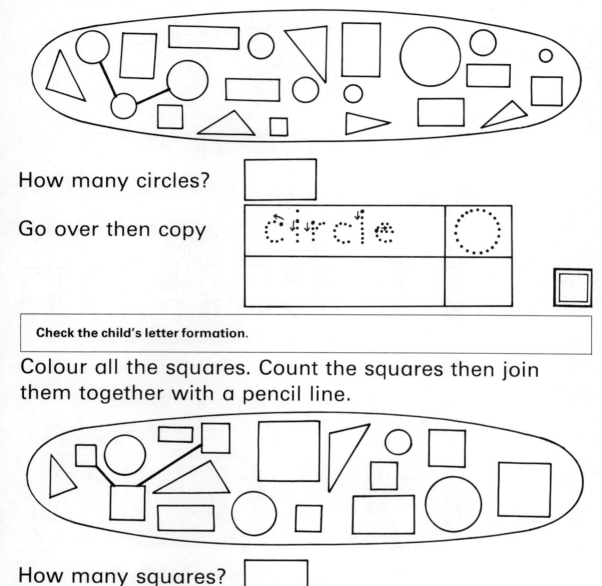

Here is a set of twelve circles. Draw one more.
How many now? | 12 |

Copy the sum about this picture.

| 12 + 1 → 13 | | → | □

Here is one square. Draw twelve more. Count the squares.
How many now? | |

Copy the sum about this picture.

| 1 + 12 → 13 | | → | □

> Don't be too fussy about perfect squares. Ask the child to read the sums aloud pointing to each number as she reads.
> Remember to look out for these shapes outdoors in pillar boxes, fences, gates, wheels. Cut out shapes from cereal packets to make shape pictures.

Colour all the triangles. Count the triangles then join them together with a pencil line.

How many triangles?

Go over then copy.

triangle

> Talk about the three sides/angles of a triangle. Test: can you make a triangle with any number of sides other than three? Allow the child to use matchsticks or straws to experiment and come to her own conclusion.

Colour all the rectangles, then count them and join them together with a pencil line.

How many rectangles?
Go over then copy.

rectangle

> A square is a special kind of rectangle. If the child spots this, see if she can find out what makes a square a square and not a rectangle. If not, don't worry about it.

Here is a set of 13 triangles. Cross one out and colour the rest.

How many triangles did you colour? ☐
Copy the sum about this picture.

| 13 − 1 → 12 | | → | | ☐ |

Draw a set of 15 rectangles. Now cross one out and colour the rest.

How many rectangles did you colour? ☐
Copy the sum about this picture.

| 15 − 1 → 14 | | → | | ☐ |

Read the sums on this page with the child. Point to each part of the sum as you read it. Give help with the last sum if needed.
MORE TO DO: Help the child to cut out six of each of the four basic shapes (different shapes can be introduced later). Use these in a snap game but instead of calling 'snap', call the name of the shape.

Put circles round the odd numbers and triangles round the even numbers. Count aloud the odd numbers, then the even numbers.

```
0   2   4   6   8  10  12  14  16  18  20
  1   3   5   7   9  11  13  15  17  19
```

Fill each bag with an odd number of sweets. Write the number of sweets you have drawn.

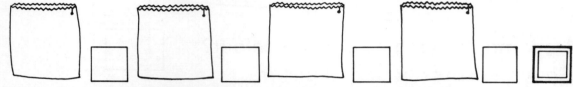

Draw <u>two more</u> marbles in each box. How many marbles now?

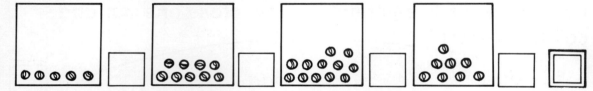

Draw +2 arrows to 20 and count aloud 'nothing add two is two', 'two add two is four'.

Draw more +2 arrows but this time start at 1.

Note the different patterns of odd and even numbers. Experiment with different adding arrows +3/+4/+5, etc. to see what happens, e.g. are the answers odd or even, or a mixture of the two?

Complete the number line.

Start at 14 and work backwards. The child can either fill in the numbers consecutively or do the odds first, then the evens (or vice versa).

Can you do these sums?

2 add 2 ⟶ ☐   1 add 2 ⟶ ☐
4 add 2 ⟶ ☐   3 add 2 ⟶ ☐
6 add 2 ⟶ ☐   5 add 2 ⟶ ☐
8 add 2 ⟶ ☐   7 add 2 ⟶ ☐
10 add 2 ⟶ ☐   9 add 2 ⟶ ☐
12 add 2 ⟶ ☐   11 add 2 ⟶ ☐

Colour green the badges which have odd numbers.

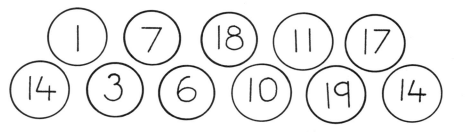

Fill in the missing links in the chain.

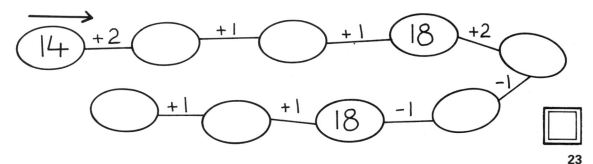

23

Draw 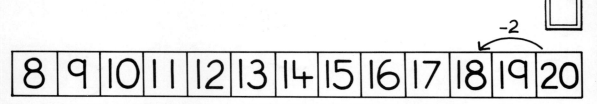 arrows and count down the number line.

| 8 | 9 | 10 | 11 | 12 | 13 | 14 | 15 | 16 | 17 | 18 | 19 | 20 |

Help the child to count aloud if necessary 'twenty take away two is eighteen', etc.

Take away two means the same as <u>less two</u>. Can you do these sums?

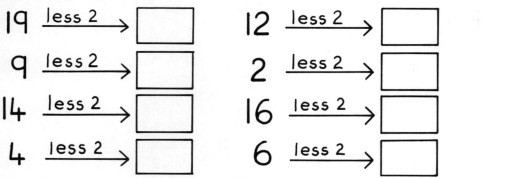

19 less 2 → ☐   12 less 2 → ☐
9 less 2 → ☐   2 less 2 → ☐
14 less 2 → ☐   16 less 2 → ☐
4 less 2 → ☐   6 less 2 → ☐

Count the buttons in each set then cross out two buttons from each set. How many now?

Fill in the missing numbers.

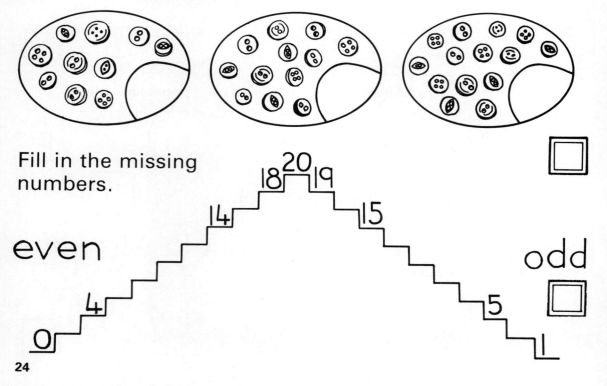

even   odd

What number comes in the middle?

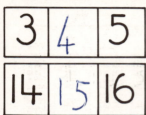

| 3 | 4 | 5 | | 17 | 18 | 19 | | 6 | 7 | 8 |
| 14 | 15 | 16 | | 11 | 12 | 13 | | 18 | 19 | 20 |

It is useful to take a number out of its usual position in a whole number line to really fix the idea of that number in the child's mind.

Write the number which is <u>one less</u> than

4 → ☐   10 → ☐   5 → ☐
14 → ☐   20 → ☐   15 → ☐
3 → ☐   1 → ☐   9 → ☐
13 → ☐   11 → ☐   19 → ☐
6 → ☐   2 → ☐
16 → ☐   12 → ☐

Complete the number chains.

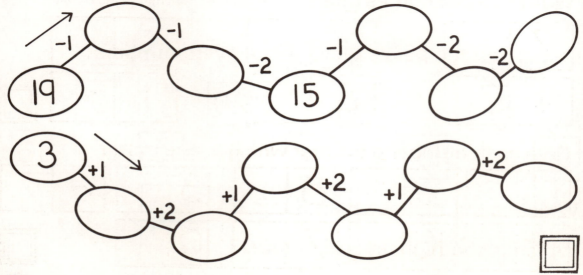

26

Go *up* the street and put <u>odd</u> numbers on the doors.

(first house door: 7)

Come *down* the street and put <u>even</u> numbers on the doors.

(last house door: 14)

What number comes <u>before</u>?

	17
	14

	13
	18

	20
	11

What number comes <u>after</u>?

7	
4	

3	
8	

10	
1	

Give each number a partner which is <u>one more</u>.

11		2		8		13		6	
19		16		7		10			

27

Complete these numbers to 20.

1	2	3	4	5	6	7	8	9	10
11	12	13	13	15	16	17	18		

> Mention that the bottom line is almost the same as the top line but with ten added to each number. Move along top line asking 4+10, 7+10, 9+10, etc. The child flicks her eye down to box below for the instant answer.

Add the ten spots in the rectangle to each of the spots in the circle, then write the answer.

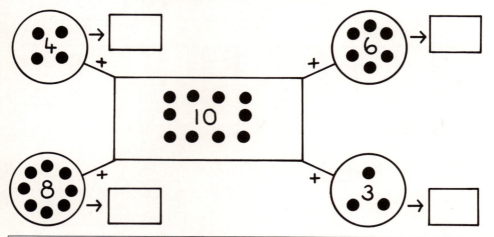

> You can reverse the process, i.e. start with the total number then subtract ten or the number in the circle.

Can you do these sums?

10 + 5 ⟶ ☐   10 + 1 ⟶ ☐
10 + 2 ⟶ ☐   10 + 7 ⟶ ☐
10 + 3 ⟶ ☐   10 + 6 ⟶ ☐
10 + 9 ⟶ ☐   10 + 10 ⟶ ☐

> These sums should not be given a lot of thought, the aim is to have an almost instant response, i.e. the child should not count in ones from ten.

Count the grapes in each bunch, then cross out 10 grapes from each bunch. How many now?

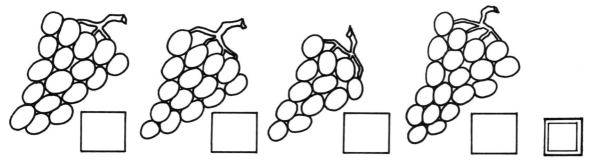

Fill in the missing numbers.

10 + ☐ → 17   10 + ☐ → 19
10 + ☐ → 14   10 + ☐ → 13
10 + ☐ → 12   10 + ☐ → 16
10 + ☐ → 15   10 + ☐ → 11

> Do the sums aloud first to check that the child is not labouring too much.

Give John thirteen balloons altogether.   Give Judy sixteen balloons altogether.

Can you write a sum about each of these pictures?

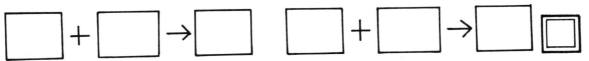

> Give help here if the child cannot see a sum in the pictures, i.e. 10+3→13, 10+6→16. Write the sum under the picture.

Read the top number chain aloud, then fill in the numbers in the bottom chain.

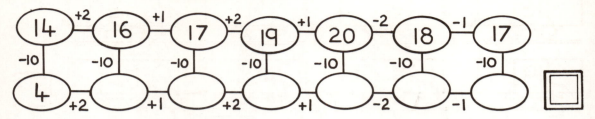

Note that the chain can be done two ways either start at fourteen and follow the instructions, or make each number in the bottom chain ten less than the corresponding number in the top chain.

Fill in the number names to finish the sum.

Ten and _____ make eighteen.
Ten and four make _____
Fifteen take away ten is _____
Three and _____ make thirteen.
Ten and _____ make sixteen.
Ten and _____ make twelve.
_____ and ten make nineteen.

Read aloud the numbers on these vests. Now add a ten to each number and read the new number aloud. Colour the vests.

Remind the child if necessary that adding ten means putting a 1 before each number.

30

Write the numbers before and after.

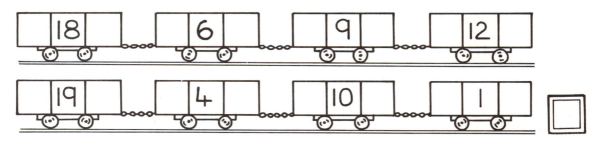

Draw twenty pigs in the field.

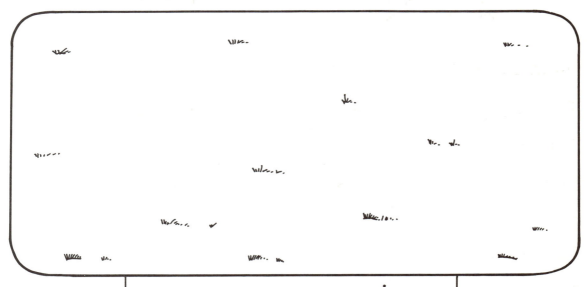

Write. twenty pigs

What is?

2 less than 4 → ☐   2 less than 14 → ☐
1 more than 15 → ☐   1 more than 5 → ☐
2 less than 12 → ☐   2 less than 2 → ☐
2 more than 8 → ☐   2 more than 18 → ☐
1 less than 20 → ☐   1 less than 10 → ☐

Join dot to dot to make the pictures.

Start at nought and go up in even numbers.

Start at twenty and count back in ones.

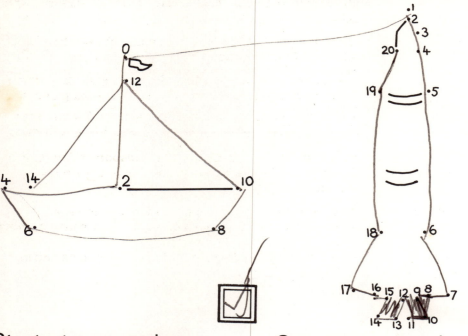

Start at one and go up in odd numbers.

Start at one and go up in ones.

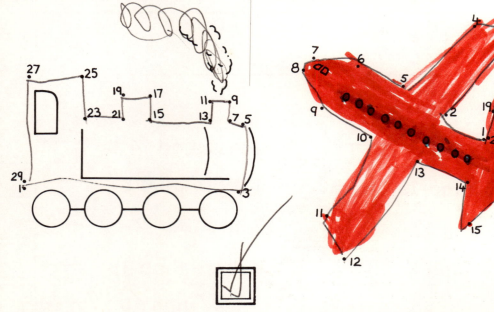

Experiment in making up your own dot to dot pictures together.